The 5 Habits of High-Performance People

Keys and scientifically proven powerful lessons for a personal change to achieve extraordinary results and reach success in life

Jason Covey

Table of Contents

Introduction

Welcome to what could be the next chapter in the greatest success of your life. The 5 Habits of High-Performance People is a book that has the potential to do more than just show how high-performance people approach their lives. As you breeze through these easy to read pages. Allow yourself to be amerced in the possibility that personal change is achievable.

Within the pages, you will find more than just self-help, this book is full of specific aspects to focus on within each chapter to drive your personal success to levels of those high-performance people you admire. The goal is to help you move from admiration to being admired. To push you out of that comfort zone and into a new area that you may not have realized you were capable of. Unleashing the possibility of new performance levels and personal growth.

It goes without saying that high performers hold themselves to a different set of standards. They care deeply about how they perform and the identity that is attached to their performance. High performers are a unique breed; they don't just perform well because they are given tasks. They perform well because the goals they set are challenging. They have a vision, and that vision is something they identify with their future. This is a contributing factor to why their drive is exponentially higher than a standard performer. It is because they are vested in being successful. They care. They are self-monitoring and evaluate their behavior and performance goals often. If a high performer is not living up to their own high standards, they re-evaluatee and adjust their behavior to get different results. High performers are able to see long term results because they have the gusto to expect great things from themselves. They repeatedly encourage themselves, and they do so with action through the achievement of goals. For a high performer having an extraordinary life is not a dream or fantasy. It is a goal a necessity even. They tie their future identities to what they want to happen and go for it.

As you journey through The 5 Habits of High-Performance People, be sure to do so with an open mind. These concepts are designed to show you just how you can level up your game and grow into more than you realize. Through this book, I encourage you to keep experimenting in life and find the thing that sparks your inner burning desire. Then alight that with your personal values and jump! Get outside your comfort zone and master things that help you become better tomorrow than you are today.

It would be remiss of me to not thank you for beginning your journey to high performance with The 5 Habits of High-Performance People. I understand that there are many options when it comes to learning about high performance in the market, so thanks again for choosing this one! Great care was taken to ensure it is full of as much useful information as possible; please enjoy it!

What we think determines what happens to us,
so if we want to change our lives, we need to
stretch our minds – Wayne Dryer

Chapter 1: Rules for Success

Individuals who are high performers typically find greater success than the rest of the crowd. To reach those levels of success, they typically follow some basic rules for success. Before we get to those rules, I want to chat with you a bit about being real with yourself.

Coaches all around the world talk about the hustle and grind to be successful. But in actuality, those concepts just beat you down. The whole concept of working so hard to achieve a goal is insane. Now that is not to say that you will not have to work at your goals, because you will. However, it's a different approach and one that high performing people use. It starts by opening yourself up to be more strategic. No more grinding, no more hustle, only thinking, and working strategically.

That is the big secret of super successful people. They use strategy in all their actions. Making the next question obvious, how do you know what to create a strategy for? How do you know where to go from here? No worries, you picked this book because you want to be a high performer, and the time has come to share all my tips, tricks, and help you build a system for success. You cannot achieve a dream without having a vision for what you want. There truly is nothing worse than waking up one morning and realizing you have been living someone else's dream. So when you think of that vision and that goal, there are a few things that a goal should do for you. It should motivate you, make you proud, scare you a tad, have a way to measure it, and set a deadline. Now, as you work through the pages of this book, let's apply your personal vision of what you want to each aspect. Take a few minutes right now and think of where you want to see yourself in 12 months. Is there a title you want? Is there something you want to accomplish? Don't worry; I will be here waiting for you to return.

Did you do it? Good! Now when you think of achieving that does it make you smile? Is the achievement of that goal a little scary? If you answered yes, awesome job on creating that vision for your future. Now it is time to think of a person. Someone you know who will hold your feet to the fire. This person will give you the hard truth when you are not living up to your potential. Do you know someone that can help you with this? Or another option would be to look at a personal coach. This is another secret that high performers have in their repertoire. It is one thing to know the steps and understand the processes; it is an entire game change to have someone that will tell you the hard truths. This period of learning how to achieve high performance is similar to that of what a child experiences. It is a complete life change. Which requires support and help. Having an accountability person often is similar to the relationship between a child and parents. The accountability person often has a much harder job than the person wishing to become high performing. This is in great part because they have to be ready to call the hard shots. To do what's right for the person seeking personal change, and not just what builds your relationship. The focus purely needs to be on accountability and growing you to achieve that vision.

As you work through the pages of this book, you will find that the implementation of systems is another secret that high performers use. It is important to start with a foundation, a grounding or baseline, some might think of these as personal commandments or rules. Before I jump right into the rules for success, take a moment and think for a bit. Think of a person who may be someone who works for you or someone on your team. You probably have no problem explaining rules and expectations to this person. Setting the standard for them to follow. For you, this may be second nature, and you thrive. It is just part of the structure or foundation of your position. Do you ever, in turn, realize that you are missing that same structure or baseline in your own tasks? Or in life? Spending your time running around, making sure everyone else is on task; everyone else is building their foundations. Hang in there it happens, it is easy to get caught up in all the things that are happening around you and become a hustler, and think your high performing when you are actually barely scratching the surface of your potential.

It's not the strongest of the species that survive,
nor the most intelligent, but the one most
responsive to change. –Charles Darwin

I have identified five rules that high performers are using to drive their success. These are really more than just rules for high performers; they truly are a form of a commandment. A non-negotiable part of the baseline for their life. The five rules for high performers are the structure, focus, income production, health, and no snooze. It is with these rules you can begin to set up your foundation for high performance. Now let us examine closer each rule individually.

Structure

Growing up, most children have some form of structure in their life. As a child, you may have been told to brush your teeth, and go to bed and wake at certain times, do homework, eat dinner, shower. Then at some point, your parents may have thought you were old enough to start making those choices on your own. They no longer provide you with a structured daily routine. Thinking you were old enough to know the things that needed to be done and would accomplish them at your own pace. Fast forward to now, you are a grown-up. What does your day look like? Do you wake up and just wing it? Do you accomplish everything you need each morning? Or are you rushing out the door with coffee in one hand and a bagel in the other. It is okay; it happens. The worse thing about winging your days is this action often results in feelings of stress, anxiety, overwhelmed, and falling short of your potential.

It is time to rethink the mindset that routines are monotonous and only for children. Using a routine to structure your day is not something that should be viewed as rigid, stifling, and boring. Quite on the contrary, a personal daily routine builds a path for productivity, happiness, freedom, success, and potential. Before I get to a sample structure for your routine, let's dive into the why structure with a routine is beneficial.

When I think of structure and routine, the concept that most stands out is efficiency. When there is a routine to follow daily, there is less need for mundane decision making. Enabling you to know what specific task needs to be accomplished without having to think. Forcing you to become more actionable in the activities you complete. This lifestyle provides you an easy transition from one activity to the next and increases your overall efficiency. As you work on the structure of this lifestyle, you will begin to build a framework of activities that are musts to complete daily. These activities will become second nature and allow you to flow into your day, rather than wing it. Additionally, the task of setting a routine helps you begin to instill good habits and work away from those that inhibit your full potential. To build good habits, you must use repetition, and that is where your routine comes to play. It takes time to develop a habit; however, as you cultivate that habit, you are building strong foundations for success. In turn, you are also removing bad habits from your life and replacing them with habits that will match your goals for the future. One of the most valuable commodities you have is your time. This asset is disposable, and once it is lost, you cannot get it back. With using a routine, you can begin to free up time that would have been wasted planning, or backtracking.

With careful structuring the design of your routine, you should begin to see a force of prioritization and importance rather than whimsically making decisions. It is quite freeing to know these are the priorities for each day. Through your routine, you will also notice that there is less willpower and determination required. The tasks in your routine will simply become rituals. It is like brushing your teeth. Nearly everyone knows each morning you need to brush your teeth, and it just happens without thinking, just simply as routine. With a ritual approach to structuring your routine. You will find that procrastination also reduces since activities become just part of the day. Subconsciously, you know I will do this for 10 minutes and move on. Procrastination is not a habit of a high performer and a thief of your time commodity. So by pushing yourself into creating these habits, you combat the urge to procrastinate. Thus, building momentum. Doing the same things each day with repetition makes it easier to be persistent. This is why starting something is hard, but the more you do it, the easier it gets. As your momentum builds, you will begin to see greater success in things you may not have realized were lacking. As you fuel those successes, you will also be fueling your self-confidence. Allowing yourself to grow and change your lifestyle into that of what you want for your future.

It is not to say that there will not be things beyond your control. It is necessary to accept that. Nevertheless, many things are within your control. Taking control of your day, in the beginning, is a great way to set yourself up for success. Aspirations and goals take time and often are not achieved all at once. Truly high performing people accomplish goals by beginning with repetition and practice. Which makes developing structuring and sticking with a routine a necessary part of moving into a high-performance lifestyle.

The structure is ultimately the most important of the five rules, and each of the other rules feeds into providing your foundation for high performance. I understand thinking of how to structure your day might seem overwhelming at this point. Where to begin? How do I know what is important, and what will help me achieve my aspirations and goals? Let us start by accepting that it takes time to become your best version. It also takes time to find the ideal daily structure to follow. So let me share with you an example of a high performer's daily routine.

Many high performers start their practice by preparing for the next day the night before. Consider this your pre-game for the next day, or planning stage. Review the things you need to accomplish and then create a plan. One highly effective method to use for this is using time blocking. Time blocking is a very simple process but highly effective. As it prevents you from multitasking and keeps you focused on the task at hand. With Time blocking, you simply block out periods of time for each thing you need to accomplish. When the time is up, you move to the next task.

Time blocking is a very successful way to keep a person on track and prevent them from distractions. Time blocking is so much more effective than to-do lists. As it is a practice of planning out the moments of your day in advance, by dedicating specific time blocks for each task or responsibility. Filling your calendar with time blocks may seem, and quite frankly, look like a chaotic mess. Yet it has quite the opposite effect. When you create a calendar with tasks of things that need to be accomplished, it is harder for other things to steal your time commodity. Time blocking works for the simple reason that humans need guides. It is easy to fall off the rails and into the black hole of social media. By scheduling out the day, high performers are able to guard against those distractions. Focusing on a single task at a single time. Which actually increases productivity up to 80% more than splitting attention. Not this is not to say that time blocking is a perfect solution. Yet, it does provide you with a structure for the day. The key here is developing a system that helps you to focus specifically on the tasks that need done and deliberately focus your attention. To start time blocking, you first want to create bookends for your day. This is the actual time you plan to start work and the actual time you plan to finish. This means if you know that your morning routine is waking up at 6 am, then you place your first-time block from 6 -7 to give you a block of time to prepare for the day. Let's say you need to be finished by 5 pm because you have to pick the kids up from daycare. So you would put the other bookend of your time at 5 pm. This helps you to prevent from working late into the evening hours and allows you to focus those hours for family, self-care, or socialization. With those bookends, you should be able to take care of your personal priorities. Now you can start focusing on the priority tasks of your day. However, there are things that you should place in between your tasks. Between each task, give yourself 5 to 10 minutes of time to allow you to switch gears and prepare for the next task. Be sure to schedule your breaks, not just your lunch, and to take them. You are more productive when you are refreshed and hydrated than struggling to just get through until lunch or dinner. High performers stick to the schedule; they also allow themselves to make mistakes. When first beginning time blocking, there is a bit of a learning curve to understand just how long tasks take. As well, they schedule an overflow day into your week. This allows them to catch up and not constantly feel behind. Ultimately it is important to understand that high performers have a plan and make time to accomplish tasks daily. They drive that plan into not just their normal work activities but their entire day.

The next task that high performers use is waking up at a time that works for you. You may hear talk of the 5 AM club, and that might work for you. However, you may also be the kind of person that needs those extra couple hours of sleep. So 10 am may allow you to start the day more refreshed and ready for work. Working 10-6 may prove to be a better fit. Now I understand this is not always an option if you have a fixed start time for your job. However, if you have the flexibility, go for it. If your start time is fixed, then look at adjusting the time you go to bed. If you know you need a full 8 hours of sleep, then consider going to bed earlier. Waking consistently at the same time each day will help cement your routine. The goal here is becoming a better you, and that will mean changes to your lifestyle.

Next, cleansing and hydrate your body. Begin your day with hydration, drinking a full glass of water that will replenish your body from the night before. Sets you on a good path of hydration. The next thing you will focus on is a fifteen-minute kick start. This may include listening to an inspirational podcast, to meditation, to gratitude for your mindset. Starting your day with these few things will continue to build repetition into your day. This is only an example of what your morning might look like. Remember, it is your day; the key here is these simple tasks: wake at the same time, hydrate, kick start.

Focus

Let us go a little deeper into the concept of focus. High-performance individuals use many different practices when it comes to this concept. One widely practiced is that of the 15-minute focus. It is important to find the method of focus that will work for you. Many high performers us meditation as their form of focus to kick start their day. This helps you to find greater self-awareness. Yet other high performers find gratitude practice to be more effective. Remember, this process is going to push you into things you have not tried before. Or maybe you have not fully committed to it.   Both of these methods can help to push you into a better mindset and prepare you for leveling up your game.

Looking closer at meditation, research shows that with just 15 minutes of meditation, a wide range of positive effects happens on the individual. These include everything from the reduction of anxiety and stress to generally better health. The practice of meditation often feels like natural medication, something that is good for you. As you get more familiar with practicing mindfulness, you will notice it is more than just something good for you. It is an opportunity to be, not to have to do anything specific simply. While there is nothing wrong with being a doer. Doing things is challenging, and thebody performs best when it can be refreshed. 15 minutes of meditation each morning can allow you clear your head of stresses, concerns, and even pain. It can help you to see the gaps that exist through relaxation and prepare you to be self-aware of your actions. One of the simplest ways to start with meditation is by using a body scan meditation.

It simply begins by finding a comfortable position to sit or lay in. Closing your eyes and begin to breathe deeply and slowly. Focusing your attention on your feet. Allow yourself to notice any stress, pain, or tension. Taking slow deep breaths allow yourself to become aware of that area of your body. As you exhale, allow the stress, pain, or tension to release from your body. Working your way from section to section of your body, continuing to breathe. Exhaling stress and tension all the way up until you reach your head.

This is just one option for meditation; the best thing is to try a variety of approaches and then stick with the daily practice that fits best for you. The important thing is not to just give up. It takes time to build a habit and see results from your efforts.

The other option many high performers choose is beginning with gratitude. The practice of gratitude seems to have nearly endless benefits. High performers who are using this practice reflect on things that they are thankful for, they feel more alive, sleep better, express more kindness, have more positive emotions, and some have even seen linked to better immune systems. These high performers do not limit their gratitude to momentous occasions. Of course, when they achieve a goal, they are thankful, but they are also thankful for simple things too. Many high performers keep a gratitude journal. This is a great way to keep this practice up for the long term. It is easy to think of standard things to be thankful for, your family, your dog, your home. However, those things will not keep your practice of gratitude fresh for long. It is essential when thinking of gratitude to focus on new things you are grateful for each day. This is why journaling is successful for those just beginning the practice. It works you slowly into changing the way you focus and ultimately perceive situations.

Using gratitude, practice changes the way you approach the world. You will begin to focus more on the good in life rather than the challenges. Now journaling isn't the only option for practicing gratitude; you need not limit yourself. If journaling begins to feel stale, try a gratitude jar, or gratitude letter, be determined to find things that you are thankful for that are not standard. Additionally, when you focus on people, you are thankful for you to move away from circumstance and materialistic thoughts. This provides you an enhancement to each experience and situation. Using this process, you become more self-aware and aware of the world around you. There are many ways to practice gratitude; you just need to seek out which is the best fit for you.

These are just two ways that high performers begin their day with focus. Regardless of what you choose and how you choose to set yourself up for the day. It is important to bring yourself to the center and focus on the potential within you for the day.

The hardest person you will ever have to lead is
yourself.
– Bill George

Income Production Activities

The next rule high performers live by is focusing on income production activities or wealth building. As I noted earlier, many high performers actually priorities their day the evening before. This prepares them for a jumpstart and hit the ground running. So they already have a plan for how to approach the day. Focusing in on IPA's (Income producing activities) help you alleviate yourself from distraction. The things that make you money are where you begin.

Morning is the best time to get productive at work, which is why unless your job revolves around email or social media, do not check it first. Never make checking your email the first objective. Rather focus on the goals for the day and knock out what really matters first. The best time of day to do creative or strategic work is the first thing.

Honestly, it is quite easy to feel like you are busy and complete a lot of things, but really rather than planning, you are reacting. Which can leave you physically and mentally depleted. So it is important to identify what are your time drains and what is actually helping you to produce more efficiently. High performers work to be as efficient as possible in every aspect of their work. They stay laser-focused on the goals for the day and crush them.

Now that is not to say that they do not check email or use social media. That is planned into their day. Allow yourself time to be social via one of your time blocks. One great way to not get sucked into hours of mindless scrolling is to set a timer and when the timer goes off, move to your next task. Another tip for email is always to leave the day with an empty inbox. When first starting out, that might be difficult, but as you work to clean out the clutter of your inbox, you will begin to see that where the priorities are, and where the time thefts are.

So how do you level up your income-producing activities? Well, it all begins with setting those goals. Your task for the day should be customized for you and your business. One suggestion some high performers use is a point system to assign activities various levels of points. So something for a client might be equal to 10 points and posting to social media zero points. This pushes you to prioritize each activity as you plan your day. So what are some examples of IPA's?

- Signing a new client
- Working on a client project
- Personal Development
- Answering Client emails

There is no perfect all-encompassing list of IPA's these will have to come from you. As each person's vision and goals are different. The key is once you decide what they are tracking them and crushing them.

One of the biggest aspects that high performers excel at is taking care of their clients and prospects. This helps to build their creditability and drive regular traffic to their lists. Once they have someone enter their community, they foster and nurture the relationship. They stay in touch with their customers using an intrinsic focus that helps them move from simple client to investor. I use the term investor loosely while it could mean that they are financially investing in the overall vision. For high performers, it also means that they are supporting more than just monetarily. This could be by sharing content or introducing the performer to additional contacts.

High performers understand the value in follow up. They use a personal connection to stand out in the crowd. They recognize that customers, clients, employees all want to know that they care. So they make the decision to send a physical card, or phone call rather than an email or text. They have found that this type of follow up helps to solidify the relationship. They understand that it's about appreciation, not self-promotion. This way, regardless of if the content changes, the relationship can survive. They use a simple guide of 20% sales-focus and 80% relationship building. They understand that everyone under the sun has a direct line to inboxes, and they cannot abuse it. So they focus the content by customizing the delivery to each person. They understand that once the relationship is built, then easing into the sales pitch happens more naturally. They understand it is all about value for the customer. So high performers find ways to share value and stand out.

Individual Health

Your personal health has a great impact on your ability to become a high-performer. Starting your day with hydration is a great way to refresh the body. Just by adding a touch of lemon juice to your water can also lower your body's acidity levels, which helps with inflammation. As well some physical activity or work out in the early morning also provides improved levels of energy and circulation. 10 to 20 minutes of exercise built into your morning routine will also help provide energy to fuel the rest of the day. It's also a great idea to have a mid-afternoon workout. It is easy to fall into an afternoon slump where your productivity drops. When high performers feel this coming on, they stop and take a 10-minute walk or do some stretches at their desks. You will be surprised how these actions can refuel you for the rest of your workday.

High performers are also conscious of what they eat. Understanding that foods you eat also play a role in individual health. We have already talked about water and staying hydrated. High performers also focus on eating a healthy mix of protein, vitamins, and slow-release carbohydrates. At breakfast, this might be an omelet, yogurt with nuts and berries, or a granola bar and fruit. When snacking, focus on snacks that provide a slow release of energy. Matching complex carbohydrates with proteins is a great option. So you might try half an apple with peanut butter. Lunch is also a contributor to that afternoon slump. Avoid food to high in fat as these will cause you to feel tired and reduce productivity. As well as for dinner, it's important to be realistic with yourself. If there are too many obstacles to create dinner, chances are you might opt for take-out. Choose dinners that do not require a lot of time or effort to put together. Or even work with a meal prep company that sends everything you need, and you just put it together.

Just as important as exercise for your health, so is taking time to relax. Allow time in your day to set aside and read, or spend time with family, or a pet. This time should be spent unwinding and reminding yourself of everything that is good in your life. High performers typically spend this time just prior to bedtime. Allowing them to come down from the day's highs and level out to begin to rest. As well many high performers also use a teaspoon of buffered vitamin c powder in their water before bed. The vitamin c helps to reduce acidity in the body, and the water, of course, helps to maintain your hydration overnight. This allows many of them to wake refreshed and with a clear head each morning. Along with this bedtime ritual, it goes to say that high performers get enough sleep. Most sleep between 6 and 10 hours. As well, to not be disturbed during the night, they also turn their phone off or to do not disturb.

They also generate the energy they are masters at transitioning between tasks and meetings. They are more likely to take a quick break to psychologically reboot and release tension than to struggle through their day unfocused. Studies have found that there is a link between health and success. That those who are using healthy habits with personal goals achieve better results. This is true for high performers as well. The University of Georgia did a study and found that in a group of 1,300 people who earned a salary of over $100,000, 75% of them said staying physically fit is part of their success routine. However, physical wellness is not the only important concept for those living a high performing lifestyle. They also take into account their social wellness. They focus on developing healthy relationships with friends and lovers. They strive to ensure that their social wellness is inline and in balance. This often means that they have stable relationships with their spouse or significant other. They thrive on the pursuit of harmony in their life.

Another concept that they foster in terms of wellness is that of their intellectual health. They have a desire to be challenged and learn from these challenges. It is with encouragement and intellectual growth that they experience mental stimulation. As an intellectual, they use all available resources to feed their needs for further development. As they grow, the continually seek learning, creative thinking, and opportunities to problem solve. It becomes almost a natural instinct for them to be up to date on current issues and their interests.

High performers permit themselves to put themselves first. To many, this sounds conceited and selfish. Yet it is about the approach the high performer uses that sets them apart. They understand their individual needs and plan for those allowing them to have the time to nurture other things in their life. But by putting their self-first, they gain strength, inner peace, motivation, and resolve to share with others. They also understand that doing too much for others can deprive them of the opportunity to find their own success. To hinder their ability to grow and develop. It is all a balance between collaborating, when to nurture, and when to go solo.

No one changes unless they want to. Not if you
beg them. Not if you shame them. Not if you
use reason, emotion, or tough love. There's
only one thing that makes someone change:
their own realization that they need to do it.
And there's only one time it will happen: when
they decide they're ready –Lori Deschene

No Snooze

Procrastination is the high performer's worst enemy. When you start out behind the curve for your day, it is hard to catch up. Which is why hitting the snooze button is the worst thing you can do. Let me explain it like this; your body naturally has a routine to wake up. Part of this routine actually starts nearly two hours before your eyes open. Your body and brain begin working together to promote wakefulness by releasing chemicals and raiding your body temperature to get you up and awake. So your body is systematically already in this process when your alarm wakes you. Hitting the snooze and going back to sleep again causes what is known as sleep inertia. This is the feeling you have of being drowsy when waking; this feeling can actually last for hours after you wake. So regardless of how good that snooze button might feel, it actually is throwing off your energy for the rest of the day.

Now, if you are already sleep-deprived, using the snooze button can make things even worse. This is because your body is already out of its routine. So when you hit the snooze button, your body can actually fall back into a cycle of full sleep. Which can actually be worse for you than waking with the first alarm. This is because of the early stages of sleep are typically the worst to wake from. They increase the feeling of exhaustion and unrest. Additionally using your snooze button regularly can actually confuse your brain. This goes back to your brain and body are working together to bring you to a state of wakefulness. By chronically hitting the snooze button, you are conditioning your brain in an unhealthy way. This is because your brain will start to think 10 more minutes of sleep rather than it is time to wake up. One way high performers combat this process is by swapping their alarm for a different kind.

There are many apps and even alarm clocks that are designed to use gradually increasing sound or light to wake you with. The great thing about these methods is they more naturally mimic the cycle of waking.

There is value in appreciating waking up. This another concept that high performers have come to realize. Much like a child is excited to wake early on Saturday and watch cartoons. As an adult, you get to choose your adventure every day. This is something high performers have mastered. They choose the adventures they choose the attitude that they bring to the day. The day is full of possibilities, rather than dreading traffic, coworkers, meetings, and did I say traffic? One way they do this is they have a reason to wake up. There is a plan, a goal, a routine. I'm sure you know when you have to catch an early flight you find it easy to wake in the morning. It's almost as if your body is tied to the alarm, and you spring awake. High performers use a similar method; they give themselves a compelling reason to wake up each and every day. They find the thing that is compelling to them. This could be learning a new language, practicing yoga, meditation. Something that they are excited to do each day. This should not be a work-related task. This is something that makes you excited to jump out of bed. Finally and maybe the most important thing is they commit. They are accountable to stay on track with their plans. They allow their coach or accountability partner to call them out when they miss that morning jog or lesson. There is great power in accountability.

Chapter 2: Principles for High Performers

As we shift from rules to live by, let's move into just how high performers achieve so much. I am a firm believer that by following the same actions of high performers, anyone can become more than they are. Before we dive into some specific principles to achieving high performance in any area, you must have clarity and belief.

The problem many faces and struggle with is being clear with what they want. Yet, typically they can clearly pinpoint what they do not want. By getting this far in the book, you clearly are ready to level up your life. I am convinced that regardless of where you currently are, in your career, launching a new venture, revitalizing a dying career, or even taking a good career to the next level, you can get there. However, before you can, you need to decide consistently to be clear with yourself, and also to make the greatest difference with results. These arnon- negotiables for pushing yourself into high performance.

When speaking about clarity, many think that it simply means accepting your limits. However, that is the wrong way to approach clarity. High performers look for potentials. They see themselves as what they can achieve; they take daily goals and work through them with detail and clarity. As well as high performers believe. This quite possibly is the thing that sets them apart from the crowd. High performers have such a strong belief in their goals; they are not afraid to take big risks to reap the rewards they know are waiting. There are many out there that will discount a dream or tell you it is not possible. It can be very easy to buy into those negative thoughts and beliefs. High performers push themselves to not buy into others' beliefs of what they can and cannot accomplish. They focus indirectly on what they want and put their effort into wholeheartedly believing in those objectives with clarity.

If you believe in what you are doing, then let nothing hold you up in your work. Much of the best work of the world has been done against seeming impossibilities. The thing is to get the work done. – Dale Carnegie

---

Accept the challenge

High performers understand that to get to the ultimate vision, and there will be a challenge. So they start with that in mind accepting that there will be a challenge to meet. Yet using the belief that they can persevere and move forward. As a high performer is working toward achieving their vision, many break things down to five things to achieve in the short term. High performers also do not work alone they have their coach or accountability partner. They may also have co-workers or employees. Regardless of who the high performer is working with, they should be clear with everyone involved in achieving the goal of what the current five challenges are. If the people working to help achieve the vision do not know where they are going, there's a great chance they could lead in the wrong direction. High performers ensure that communication of the challenge is clear. However, sometimes this can be challenging itself. They work hard to ensure that the heartbeat of the vision is understood at all levels.

There is power within expectations. Individuals who achieve great things understand that sometimes expectations even take on their own language. It is more than just words. Even the unconscious assumptions feed into the words they use.

Think of it this way. Two individuals use the exact same words to achieve their goal, yet; they come up with different results. This is because of the influence of one's expectations versus others. High performers have high expectations for their results. They expect what they desire and see the correlation between expectation and desire. The single greatest skill a person can possess is the ability to achieve meaningful goals. Those who are high performers have found the bridge between action and expectations. Those who are high performers also have a burning desire to be actionable about their goals. As well, they meld their actions to meet the expectations they have set for those goals. Creating a one-two punch and giving them the upper hand in success.

Life is about accepting the challenges along the way, choosing to keep moving forward, and savoring the journey.
–Roy T. Bennett

High performers understand that they need to seek out the clarity that often it will not just come to them. Many successful people do not wait until the new year to self-evaluate; they decide when to make changes along the way. Constantly seeking out clarity and squashing distractions.

Be Honest

High performers can handle being told the hard cold truth about business and their performance. The truth I often what they need to level up, and they insist on having it. For high performers, feedback is important. High performers want specific and focused feedback on their actions. This is the only way to move forward to meet their goals. Feedback like "lacks focus" isn't actionable, and would not help push them to the next level.

High performers also use specific anchors for the development of their character. Which requires them to take an honest approach to their lives. These anchors are the power to act and the power to choose. Both of which require the individual to be brutally honest with him or herself. Since high performers focus on being proactive, they set themselves up to also choose the attitude in which they approach situations. Attitudes are a free choice for everyone, you can choose to rise above, or you can choose self-doubt. Those killing it as a high performer consciously make a choice every day to act upon this freedom of choice and choose to approach life with a positive attitude.

The last of human freedoms is to choose one's attitude in any given set of circumstances. – Victor Frankl

---

It is with all of these things in mind that high performers cultivate a practice of using feedback to build on their success. As well they seek out the challenges and face them head-on. They are honest with their performance and have a team of those who support them that are equally as honest. Even when things are not what they wish to hear, they adjust and refocus to get back on track for that ultimate goal of their vision.

High performers believe that authenticity is key to developing an honest relationship. It is not to say that sometimes it takes a lot of courage to be honest. The natural tendency for people is to move as far away from pain as they can. High performers do not simply develop honest relationships externally but also internally. They listen to their inner voice as well; they listen to their moods and determine which voice is at the forefront. They work to accept the reality of situations and self-guide to different solutions. They are truthful, most of all, with themselves. They do not lie and say things are perfect when they need work. They tell themselves the hard truth that they could work harder, or they could have acted differently. They use these moments of truth with their self to bring positivity into their lives. They are vigilant against the negativity and solution-driven.

Future Focus

High performers rarely look far into the future and think about what they need. Rather they focus on the current needs and achieving the current goals. It is with these short term goals that they know will build into their vision that they can focus and feel successful. High performers are constantly evolving and scouting for solutions and new talent. The focus on having the right talent in the right positions. They continue to learn and grow, keeping up to date with new skills and considering new opportunities. They use each challenge that they face as a learning opportunity and focus on what that challenge can provide as an opportunity for the future.

High performing people understand the importance of continuous advancement. They often take charge of their own

Personal development. They look for every opportunity to advance their skills, and they do not limit themselves to those options available with their company. May participate actively in conferences, seminars, and other outside learning opportunities. High performers are always looking to grow with each new challenge.

Additionally, high performers realist that to build a future-focused group, they need to be flexible and resilient. They need to focus on the competencies and strengths of their self and their team. The key is constantly enhancing efficiency and encouraging outstanding performance. They develop a culture of clear values and with the specific purpose of boosting their team and self. They work to ensure that the vision is clear and that the mindset of their team is open and ready to innovate. They can feel the overall pulse of their business or vision and are committed to building new skills and talent.

High performers understand that development and learning approaches must meet the specific needs and expectations that align with the goal or vision. They have a strong desire to acquire new capabilities and skills. They also work to grow their character and core values. They see that the key to this is newly learned skills, competencies, and knowledge to utilize and apply immediately. They have a commitment to farther strengthen their knowledge and continuously develop. They foster a culture that is focused on new skills and growing talent. Not only do they look to grow in their industry or to enhance their vision. They also look to build personal and social competencies. As inner self-worth is a valuable commodity. They constantly expand their relationship and encourage others to do so as well.

Don't limit yourself. Many people limit themselves to what they think they can do. You can go as far as your mind lets you. What you believe, remember, you can achieve. –Mary Kay Ash

---

Open to Communication

High performers seek honesty in the communication they receive. They also expect a level of trust in their actions. Their communication style is transparent, and they do not want to be ignored. This type of communication helps them to see where they are successful and where the next challenge might be. When high performers are communicated with, they like to use SMART goals (specific, measurable, achievable, relevant, and time-bound). While high performers do not want to be micromanaged, they do crave engagement and challenges. High performers often become key at helping define strategy. They crave to find the solution to the problem and then implement it.

High performers are often specific in their communication style. They have a goal or challenge and are focused on results. This leaves little time in the high performer's communication for meaningless communication. They are deliberate and professional with each contact. High performers often prefer email or text communication as they are able to get directly to the point and then move on. This is not to say that high performers are abrupt, rude, or short. They just simply like to move forward with concise clarity within their communications.

Now while they do like to be clear and concise in communication, they also enjoy building their network. This is the time when the high performer gets outside of the current challenge and works to develop relationships to grow their visions. Ultimately for the high performer, it is all about getting to the next level, and that often requires a village of people to help them drive their success. Likewise, high performers know the value of saying goodbye. One benefit of clear commination is that everyone knows where the challenges are and the strategy to get there. When a high performer is faced with the realization that their goals are not aligning with the company or process, they know when to say goodbye. They have the courage to reevaluate how the current situation aligns with their vision and make the hard choice of going forward or hitting the restart button. They are capable of shifting gears to ensure that they meet their goals and drive their own success. They also are not afraid to bring to their manager or supervisor issues that are preventing them from getting to that next level.

High performers are also very authentic in their communications. They must inspire truthful, fully transparent, honest, and open communications. They encourage a level of safety and comfort at a psychological level. This allows them to address tough issues and challenging problems to enhance their teams. Additionally, they realize the value in time for self-reflection. That self-reflection often leads to self-discovery. With is crucial in cultivating the ability to be open-minded when receiving feedback. Allowing them to listen actively and not feel emotional in responding. Developing a strong ability to communicate is essential. As well it is necessary to be able to be communicated with. To be able to take the hard criticism and not see it as judgments of character, but allow it to push you to be a better version of yourself. High performers use communication as a two-way street, seeing that there is no value in animosity of feedback.

As high performers evolve, they are learning that there is always a need for courageous collaboration and to build strong relationships. The power in connections and confidence in others helps to push them to higher levels of performance. They understand the need to personalize their world and share ideas and insight. They effectively collaborate and use their team to intensify meaningful work. Using open two-way communication.

Unleash Capability Rather Than Control

High performers understand clearly that power does not come from control. They are aware that this is simply an illusion and that those using a controlling style for their team or employees often lead to an unfavorable reputation. As well they know that it is a much less effective way of motivating and engaging those who are helping to achieve the ultimate vision. High performers know that real power is found through engagement. They have learned through challenges or intuitively know that when you empower those around you, you foster an environment of value. This provides them with a team of people who want to gain traction and move the goal forward.

High performers are selective in their choices; they hire the right people. This is important because there are many out there that simply just want to be told what to do and are not vested in being empowered. Those people actually undermine the performance of high performers. High performers are looking for team members who have a desire for success, and show results. Ultimately they screen the team prior to beginning the challenge and asses each member's level of commitment. Then work from there to develop a plan to either encourage success or release the underperformer.

High performers have no problem releasing control once clear communication has been given. They are not here to control every decision. They focus on ensuring the right person is in the right place. Yes, they provide guidance and weigh in on issues, but ultimately they are working to create the vision and see that the challenge is being met. They see the relationship with their team as more of a partnership rather than a simple delegation. Anyone can be delegated to, but when you layer in partnership, you allow the other individual to have responsibility and feel valued in their role. Within each challenge, a high performer faces to meet their vision; there are always steps to accomplish that challenge, and those are the roles that the team provides. Allowing them to gain traction and ensure that they have value helps to increase their individual accountability for tasks and pushes the high performer to grow as a leader. High performers see the building of their team not as losing power but gaining. As those who can do things as good as or better than they can only increase the team's overall performance.

A company's job isn't to empower people...
It's to remind people that they walk in the
door with power and create the conditions for
them to exercise it. –Patty McCord

Chapter 3: Habits for High Performance

Many possess the desire to succeed, yet few have the burning desire to change. High performers are able to grab success because they have identified habits that guide them on their journey. Perception plays a large role in how high performers view the world. In any given situation, high performers seek the challenge and welcome changing their perception for success.

Successful performers might use their character to push for success. Character traits of these individuals include integrity, courage, temperance, and humility. These character traits might include things like humility, integrity, courage, and temperance. High performers have shifted that push from success beyond their character to a personality. These personality traits include behavior, attitude, and image. High performers are not necessarily interested in quick fixes, simply to save time. They believe quick fixes are simply Band-Aids for a short-term solution to the challenge. With this in mind, they focus their teams on shifting their habits into solving the problem, not just fixing it.

High performers assert that they are in charge. They choose the script of their life. It is through self-awareness that they take responsibility and are proactive in their decisions. They foster the ability to examine their character and decide how to view situations and their personal character. This ability allows them to control just how effective they are. In simple terms, they see the value that being proactive has on effectiveness. This is a major difference between those who are reactive. You see, reactive people understand that there is a problem, but they do not seek out the problem. They wait for the problem to fulfill the prophecy then react. Whereas, proactive people seek out the problem. They use not just responsibility but "response-ability" to solve problems before they have to react.

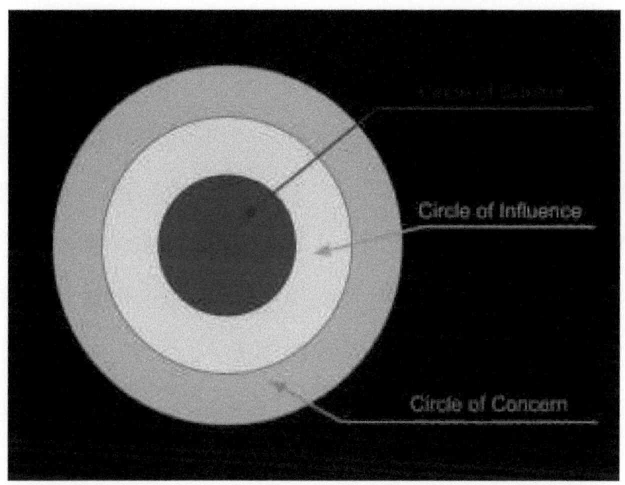

High performers use an arrow out approach to these problems. Understanding that they gain strength from the positive energy they have within their circle of influence. The circle of influence is basically the things that you can do something about. Whereas the challenge or issue is the circle of concern. The arrows out approach allow the performer to push positivity and seek solutions. While the arrows in approach are more reactive, which puts the performer into a negative spiral, often feeling like the victim. Shifting thinking to solution thinking and proactivity is another way that high performers boost their processes. Let's go a little deeper into the concept of concern, influence, and control.

To best understand how high performers work though this concept developed by Stephen Covey. I like to use this diagram. Feel free to create your own as we go through the next bit. High performers use these circles to categorize their challenges. They start by working with their team or individually to draw a large circle on a sheet of paper. This circle will represent the circle of concern. Within that circle, they place sticky notes of all the areas of concern they have for a specific project. They include everything from how they feel to needs. Next, draw a smaller circle inside the middle of the large circle; this is the circle of control. These would be all the things they can actually control. They move the things that they can actually control from concern into control. Many will feel that there are items that are out of their control, and this causes stress and anxiety. So we draw another circle between concern and control, and we call that influence. This is where we question those things that we feel are out of our control and look at is there a way we can influence a different result. The goal is to move all the notes from concern to either control or influence. This often provides an opportunity for self-discovery and innovative solutions.

The circle of influence tool is one that high performers use consistently. They question all the things that they feel are a concern and work to develop ways that they can influence or control the situations. They also understand that there are some things outside their control and are left with simple awareness that they cannot affect them, but they find relief in acknowledgment of these situations.

The vision of the high performer is what guides them to decide the value. With this in mind, they begin each challenge with the end in mind. Understanding that it is easy to busy yourself. High performers evaluate the concept of business and understand if a task really matters. This is how they know to take steps that really matter and lead them in the right direction.

It's incredibly easy to get caught up in an activity trap, in the busyness of life, to work harder and harder at climbing the ladder of success only to discover that it's leaning against the wrong wall. – Stephen Covey

These high performers use self-awareness to shape their lives; they do not focus on the standard or default preferences of others. They are the makers of their lives. Additionally, they understand their center. This is the source of wisdom, guidance, security, and power. This center is a fundamental part of their life and determines motivation, actions, decisions, and even interpretation of events. High performers have many different centers. Some find their center in self by being secure in the contestant changing and shifting of view of the world, and how circumstances, events, or decisions affect them. Others may be a family-centered with a foundation in family acceptance and fulfilling the expectations of their family. Traditions and family models often guide Their actions.

Others may be pleasure centered. This is to say the center themselves on what gives them the greatest pleasure. They see the world in terms of what gives them the greatest amount of pleasure. These centers fundamentally guide their daily motivations, actions, and decisions. Additionally, high performers also approach their center with principle, aligning beliefs, and values with behaviors. This leads to high performers maintaining the exceptional discipline to focus on their challenges and goals. They have to have the willpower to do things even when they don't want to. They focus on acting in accordance with their values rather than impulse and desire.

The high performer often is an empathic listener. They seek to understand the challenge before offering a solution. In order to be effective in this way, they have to learn to listen. Yet it is more than just listening. An empathetic listener is an inspiring characteristic. It requires a fundamental shift in the paradigm. It means the individual no longer seeks to be understood, yet they listen with the intent to understand, not simply reply. As an empathetic listener, they evaluate what is said, then probe to ask questions for a frame of reference. Then give counsel to advise based on their personal experience. Finally, they try to figure out the motives or behavior based on their own motives. This gives high performers a deeper understanding of other's needs and increases their credibility.

They also understand that there is value in differences. The perspective of another person provides the opportunity to uncover possibilities that they may not have considered. Embracing this allows them to see value in differences and expand perspective. It also helps to remove negativity from potential preconceived notions and look for the good in others. As well, it enhances their courage and ability to be interdependent on others, encouraging them to be open. As they become more open, they open themselves to solutions that those with a closed perspective may not have even thought possible.

Additionally, high performers understand that they must devote time to renewing themself mentally, spiritually, physically, and socially. It is through this renewal that they can take all the concepts of the seven habits and increase performance. High performers are aware that there are four areas that each requires balance. Mentally they continuously expand their mind. They do this through reading, journaling, and using enriching programs. Spiritually they focus on their values with reinforcement of the commitment of the system at their core. This could be through meditation, prayer, being in nature, or reading. Physically they ensure to renew themself by sufficient rest, eating well, and building endurance. Lastly, they renew themselves socially by developing meaningful relationships. They seek to understand other people deeply. As they focus on renewing and working to embrace positivity. They look to be an inspiration to others through empathy and by encouraging proactivity.

Habit 1 – Value in Time

High performers understand that not all uses of time are equal. This simple truth is part of what sets them apart from standard performers. Those performing at high levels spend their time focusing on more profitable work. They spend their time investing in people to build relationships. Creating flexible careers and enjoy more freedom. As well they typically contribute more to society. They have accomplished all this because they know how to manage time on a daily basis effectively.

High performers also understand their own value. They have an internal gauge for how much their time is worth. They have an intrinsic ability to know if a task is worth their time. At all levels of performance, people make choices to decide if things are worth their time. Even if it is as simple as do I pay a lawn service to cut the grass to save one hour of time. Is my time worth $40 to have the service? We all make choices like these every day. However, the majority of people base their decision on feelings or guesswork rather than actual calculations. High performers truly weigh out the value of what the hour is worth. If they can put that same hour of cutting the grass into personal development, closing a deal, or self-care then it may be worth the $40 to have the grass cut by someone else. Each person has to determine their own personal value.

High performers do not waste time focusing on things that are not in the scope of their vision. They focus on what they want and know the core values to achieve it. They also understand that the value of free time is non-negotiable. It is easy to begin calculating the value of your time and pushing yourself to work more hours. High performers understand that there cannot be a monetary value set to their free time. This time rewards them for the hours of work they have already done. These rewards can be anything from enjoying music to volunteering within the community. High performers that want to set a value for a free time give it a value based on the level of happiness or meaningfulness the task adds to their life.

Furthermore, they focus on the value of time management. This is one quality they take very seriously. This is because they understand that time is limited; there is a finite amount of time each day. So they work to ensure that they consistently use the time they have to the best of their abilities. They also understand that when they take control of their time, they improve their ability to focus and accomplish more with less time. Regardless of the method they use for blocking time or list-making, they quickly can see that they have greater momentum and improved decision-making abilities. High performers understand that without structure and a plan for their time, it is way too easy to just jump into decisions and not have time to assess the best option. By using effective time management, they are able to improve their decision-making skills and avoid stress in many situations. This is not to say that emergencies do not arise, but that they are better prepared in those situations because every decision is not a reaction. This allows them to be in greater control of their day and ultimately push towards achieving their vision.

If you don't value your time, neither will others. Stop giving away your time and talents. Value what you know & start charging for it. – Kim Garst

---

Habit 2 – Power of the Plan

Research shows that only about 3% of Americans take time and effort to plan for the future. Of that 3%, they accomplish five to 10 times that of the other 97%. The majority of people actually spend more time planning a vacation than they do the goals for their life. High performers understand the importance of planning at all levels. They are comfortable to plan and implement the plan because it reminds them of the goal and ultimate vision. With a plan, there is a course of action to take, and it is the most efficient way. High performers inherently know the value of planning and the risks when there is no plan. They also understand that planning does not always require lots of time and work. It is because of the shift in the perceptions that they can see that planning helps to increase efficiency. The basics of the plan should include:

- Where am I starting?
- Where do I want to be?
- What will it take to get there?

High performers begin by establishing a baseline for where they currently are. It is with this information they can measure the progress they are making. Depending on the challenge, this might be very straight forward. Yet it can also be more of a reflective question. Regardless of where high performers realize, it is critical to acknowledge and identify where they are starting. So, for example, let's say I have 10 clients, and my goal is to double my business.

The next thing they look at is where do they want to be? This is simple enough; if they know where they are then, they should know what the goal is. So as with the previous example, I know my goal was to double my business. So I would need to get 10 to 15 new clients to double the business or a major contract. The next thing the high performer would do is look at the steps to get to that goal. What challenges are going to be part of achieving that goal? Then they look at the specific actions to implement the goal and overcome any challenges that might get in the way. They are sure to include start and end dates. They also share the plan and challenges with those they are working with. Everyone should be aware of the challenges and all working towards the same goal.

In addition to working to achieve the success of our ultimate vision. Planning allows us to move on to other things as well. Once the plan is made, the high performers can stop thinking about the single goal or challenge and make room for other opportunities. Look at planning as pre-decisions. The key with these is they put the cue in place for action and allow high performers to go after their goal unconsciously. It frees up cognitive resources to think beyond the current moment. This gives the high performer the freedom to see more than what is in front of them and go for bigger goals driving their success towards that ultimate vision.

Our goals can only be reached through a vehicle of a plan, in which we must fervently believe, and upon which we must vigorously act. There is no other route to success. –Pablo Picasso

---

Habit 3 – Daily Enrichment

High performers understand that there is great value in enriching each day. Specifically, they understand that reading can have a significant benefit in different areas of their persona. Studies have shown that daily reading increases brain

Activity by keeping the brain engaged and active. They see the brain just like any muscle in their body. Understanding that their brain requires exercise to stay healthy and strong. High performers use reading to keep their brains sharp, but they also play games like chess or even do puzzles to up their cognitive stimulation.

They also recognize that no matter how much they go into the day with a positive attitude, there will still be stress. Stress in their career, in relationships, in many day-to-day challenges in life. Some use reading as a way to escape, allowing themselves to get lost in a great story. Or by reading an engaging article to distract them and keep them present at the moment. This is why you see many commuters on the train reading. It is a form of cognitive stimulation but also provides them a moment to get out away from their stresses.

Additionally, they understand that everything they read has the potential to fill their brain with new knowledge. They know that they are better equipped to tackle new challenges, that they may have never considered facing. As well they understand that the more they read, the more expansive their vocabulary becomes. One skill that high performers possess is the ability to be well-spoken and articulate. This skill is useful in any profession. It builds on their credibility; if they sound like they know what they are talking about, and speak with confidence, people listen. It is widely known those who are well-read are knowledgeable on a wide range of topics and can engage in many situations. They also understand that the knowledge they gain is the one thing that no one else can ever take from them. Beyond increasing vocabulary and general knowledge. High performers benefit by reading; they exercise their memory. Through reading, you are exposed to an assortment of backgrounds, characters, history, nuances, and ambitions. Not to forget subplots in each story. This helps to flex your memory allowing your memory to forge new synapse while strengthening existing brain pathways.

Performers at all levels can benefit from enrichment or continuing education. High performers recognize that investing time into self-improvement is rewarding. That though education, they advance their qualifications and position for success. As well high performers know what they need to get where they want. They seek out the requirements for the position and drive their performance to exceed those requirements. Some positions may require advanced degrees or certifications. This is where high performers set themselves apart. They stand out and impress hiring managers by having the qualifications to handle the responsibilities of the specific positions they are seeking. High performers understand that there is also a direct correlation between that of those who have advanced education. Those who have a college degree typically also earn twice the amount of those without. This also feeds into when high performers feel an opportunity not working out

For them. By having education and skills that come with credentials, they are better equipped to transition positions within the company or elsewhere. It is with these credentials that they become more marketable to prospective clients or employers. In competitive environments, it is essential to stand out from the crowd. They recognize that having relevant and current insights into trends and technology levels up their game. This is the biggest reason high performers focus on allowing themselves to gain knowledge daily. Yet, they still keep their pulse on growing as a person. They have found that through personal growth, they are better equipped to deal with situations.

As a high performer, it really is about commitment. However, sometimes it is hard to know where to start. So I have found a few ways to help you increase your general knowledge each day. This is not to say that you need to do each of these every day, but add them into your routine. Each are available with just a couple clicks of your mouse or taps with your finger.

The first is to subscribe to the "Featured Article" list on Wikipedia. Each day a new article is selected from the amazing repository of entries. Wikipedia then sends this article to subscribers. As a subscriber, you will be exposed to a wide range of information from why Kazakhstan no longer uses daylight savings time to why daylight savings time was proposed during World War I as a way to conserve coal usage.

Growing general knowledge helps high performers set themselves apart and prepare for any conversation.

The second is subscribing to the free dictionary's feed, or visit their homepage. They offer this day in history, news, and article of the day. This is also a great way to level up your vocabulary by learning the word of the day each day. Challenging yourself to use these newly learned words in your conversations throughout the week. With just a few minutes, you can feed your brain with interesting facts and grow your vocabulary.

Thirdly it is important to understand that in many cultured societies, art is an important topic. To gather additional understanding or learn more about different artworks, you install on your phone the app daily DailyArt or follow them on Twitter. This is a great way to get a look at different versions of art, along with exposure to cultures you may not have ever accessed. The greatest thing about using the app is it also provides you with the story. You will receive information about the painters and the painting each day.

> The purpose of art is washing the dust of daily
> life off our souls —Pablo Picasso

Finally, one of what I believe is the best way to increase your knowledge and growth is through TEdTalks. These are short videos that you can listen to on your commute or even while getting ready in the morning. They provide you with a gamut of options for growing your knowledge base. They also help you shift perspective and become a better listener. All of these things are skills that high performers use daily. They understand that without growth, there is decay. It is by pushing yourself to the limit in balanced ways that they can achieve their visions.

Habit 4 – Self Care

There is an entire group of workers that simply believe that when it comes to productivity, the key to getting ahead is more work. More clients, more time, more work, just more everything. This way of thinking can make success feel impossible. It can cause the individual to lose hope of ever achieving their vision. Feeling so burnt out that they give up. The old concept that successful people have to be stubborn, sleep-deprived, borderline manic people obsessed with profits and neglectful of their self-care has shifted. While I am sure many people might still fill this category. Those truly high performers have shifted out of this stereotype and actually understand that it is harmful and discourages it from their peers.

High performers understand that taking time to care for themselves emotionally, mentally, and physically is a necessity. They see the value in balancing the challenges they face day to day with the importance of caring for themselves. Balance is definitely a quality that separates good performers from high performs. Those that can achieve this understand that by finding this balance, they are enhancing their leadership qualities. As well they know that failing to find balance is a strategic failure, which can spill over into the rest of their work. High performers understand that they need to focus, think, and support others is necessary to achieve their goals. Ignore the needs of your body to rest, reset even actually hurts these abilities. When you engage in self-care, it actually boosts the spirit, mind, and body, which actually boosts your cognitive processes.

So what actually is self-care? So wipe those visions of days at the spa, bubble baths, and cucumbers on the eyes. While yes, those could be all things you might do, it is so very much more than this. Self-care is specific and deliberate actions you take to support your emotional, physical, and mental health. So while you can include those relaxation techniques of a spa day as self-care, it can also be a walk outside, chatting with a supportive friend, or finding a good book to read. At the core of self-care is building one of the most important relationships you will ever have. It is the relationship with yourself. The connection between you and yourself mind, body, and spirit. Self-care is truly about giving yourself the things you need. When you understand yourself and allow yourself to bloom, this relationship can take you to the happiest level. In turn that happiness can also drive your productivity. Research shows that high performers who practice self-care actually have a higher level of cognitive ability; they also focus and concentrate for longer periods. Thus increasing overall productivity. Let's look a little closer at some ways high performers use self-care to improve performance.

The importance of getting enough sleep cannot be stressed enough. There is a huge correlation between sleep and productivity. If you do not get enough sleep, productivity actually takes a nosedive. A study was conducted on workers who suffered from insomnia or poor sleep actually spend three times as long on time management during the day. Sleep deficient workers also report trouble with focus, memory, decision-making, and lack of motivation. Some studies have even found that the lack of sleep actually causes a similar experience in the prefrontal cortex as abuse of alcohol. In some instances, sleep-deprived individuals actually are operating as if they are drunk.

High performers understand that by getting enough sleep, they are setting their days up for a better experience. Many high performers start their routine slowly and ease into relaxation. Specifically, they turn off anything that can emit blue light. This would include phones, tablets, TVs, and any type of screen device. The screen from these devices actually emits a blue light that inhibits the body's ability to produce melatonin, a sleep hormone. They each have their own routines that are built into their day. The evening could look like a relaxing bath or shower. Changing into pajamas. Dimming of the lights and reading a physical book. These practices high performers have found incorporating into their bedtime routine are successful. However, as you journey to become a high performer, find the right routine for you and be consistent with it.

High performers also understand that to get to this powerhouse position, and they have to put their phone down. It is a transition from the thinking that the secret to success is walking around with the world in your pocket, the truth is putting the phone down is the best thing you can do for your happiness, and productivity. Smartphones are one of the biggest culprits of time theft. They give off the sensation that they are helping you get more done, but they actually could be tanking your productivity. They are a massive distraction; the average person gets greater than 50notifications each day. Each time the phone buzzes, it can take up to 23 minutes to refocus and get back in the productivity zone. Now let's be real; I am not saying high performers throw away their phones. However, they understand that putting the phone down and stepping away has value. High performers do not stay connected 24 hours a day. They understand that part of self-care is setting the phone down. High performers have found that they have the greatest success with stepping away from that distraction by putting their phone in a drawer or even in a different room. This allows them to focus on the tasks at hand and not be tempted to look at their phone. They also understand that scheduling screen-free time every week and focusing on engaging in life, relationships without technology connects them back to the people they care for. Turning your phone off before is another great practice this way, it will not negatively impact your sleep. As well as remove distracting apps from your phone. This way, when you have downtime, you are not as likely to pick up your phone to use. This will keep you both professionally and personally, at the moment. There is great power in stepping away from your phone. It can allow you to be present, engaged, and that definitely is a form of self-care.

It's not selfish to love yourself, take care of
yourself, to make yourself happy. Happiness is
a priority, and it is necessary
–Mandy Hale.

Self-care does not mean high performers are selfish. It is actually the opposite. Through the practice of self-care, they are actually able to do more for their families, employees, and teams. Through the practice of self-care, they position themselves to provide support through their own experience;

they can provide examples for employees to manage stress. They also have more energy to help others. It is through using these restoration practices that leaders are reducing their own stress and able to commit to continuous improvement.

Another thing high performers do well is staying present. It is easy to stress about the future or the past. Doing these things prevents you from being present in the here and now. High performers understand that one of the best ways they can care for themselves is by bringing attention to the moment. Many use mindfulness in meditation. Mindfulness is a practice of bringing your attention to focus on the present moment. They out a few minutes each day to bring attention to the present moment. This small act of self-care has boosted the performance of many. People who practice meditation have found great benefits of increased focus, improved memory, and decreases in stress and anxiety. Some research has shown that mindfulness meditation can change the structure of the brain for the better. Those who practice meditation show an increase in gray matter density in the section of the brain for learning and memory. They also have shown a decrease in the gray matter density of the brain's stress response and anxiety sectors. One of the greatest things about meditation is it does not take years to begin to see changes. Those who begin often see improved cognitive functions in as little as two weeks.

Self-care is important to drive productivity, but how do you start? If you are not currently using self-care in your routine. It is time to level up and get you on the road to consistent self- care in your daily life. Understand that the beginning is as easy as you make it. The point is to make time for yourself, to allow you the freedom to accomplish more, not less. So the last thing to do is get to the point where self-care feels like just another task on the never-ending to-do list. Begin by making a date with yourself. Put it on the calendar, add it a time block. Then follow through with it. Let me say that again, follow through with it. You have to be willing to try new things to find out the best practice for you. So be open to trying new things. That is the beauty of self-care; there are so many things you can do. Look at each of these things as the thing that will make you feel better. When you feel better, you will increase your productivity. So find your thing and level up.

As you grow into this new space of self-care, be cautious that you do not slip out of self-care mode. Be aware of yourself with compassion. Be authentic with yourself. Some signs that you have lost touch with yourself may include

Self-neglect, allowing your workload to overflow your plate. It can become a pattern for many standard performers. This is the feeling of always running behind, increased anxiety, and difficulty maintaining composure during minor interruptions. This can lead to complete burn out.

Maintaining a specific persona can be an important skill, but in some cases, you may be over self-managing. It is possible to over-manage yourself; when you do this, you are not your authentic self. You end up working hard to uphold this fake "professional" game face. Which is exhausting, inauthentic, and cannot last. Remember, high performers are authentic; they are true to themselves, and others respect and trust this in them. Always work for genuine authenticity.

Habit 5 – Concentrated Focus

Concentration and focus can be difficult to achieve. Many want to learn how to improve in both areas. However, accomplishing it is not an easy task. The world we live in is noisy and full of constant distractions making it hard to focus. High performers understand that honing both of these skills is necessary. There is a lot of science around the concepts of sharpening your mind and focusing on what matters.

High performers understand a very basic concept, and that is to focus on something that means you have to ignore other things. They understand that focus can only happen with they have said yes to one option; this means denying all other options. In essence, what you do not do decides what you can do.

> What you don't do determines what you can do
> –Tim Ferriss

Obviously, the focus is not permanent cannot do, but it is a present that cannot do. High performers understand that they always have the option to pick back up something later, but in the present, they must focus on the specific thing at hand. With this, they understand that the key to productivity is a focus because they have said no to all other tasks they have unlocked the ability to accomplish what is left.

So why do high performers have such an inherent ability to focus? Well, it is not necessarily that most people have trouble focusing; more say they have trouble deciding. Humans clearly have the ability to focus, yet distractions get in the way. It is like when there is a deadline, and you absolutely have to get it done. It may have been easy to procrastinate beforehand, but now it is urgent, and you were forced to make the decision. Rather than choosing one thing to focus on, many make the mistake of thinking or convincing themselves that multitasking is a better option.

Multitasking is not the better option; it is actually very ineffective. Yes, technically, we can do more than one thing at a time. It is possible to cook dinner and watch TV, or answer an email and be on the phone. However, what is not possible is concentrating on two tasks at the same time. Concentration cannot be divided. With multitasking, you are actually causing your brain to switch back and forth very quickly. This would not be an issue if the brain had seamless transitions, but it does not.

If you have ever been in the middle of writing something and someone interrupts you, then when the conversation is over, you go back to the message, and it takes a few seconds to get back on track. This is essentially what multitasking is doing to your brain. The jump from one task to another has a metal cost. In psychological terms, it is called switching cost. The switching cost is what we experience in performance disruption when we switch focus from one area to another. A study found that the average person checks there email every five minutes. Of that time, it takes 64 seconds to get back to the previous task after check email. So in just email alone, the average person wastes one out of every six minutes.

So how do high performers overcome these multitasking tendencies and focus on one thing at a time? One method that some high performers use was derived by the famous investor Warren Buffett. This method uses a 2 list strategy to approach what needs to be accomplished. It is a very simple 3-step strategy for productivity. That helps the high performer to determine actions and priorities. It is a great way to commit to doing one thing the right way and help with decision making. If you would like, you can grab a paper and complete the process as you read.

Step 1: Begin by writing down the top 25 goals for the week.
Step 2: Now review this list and circle the top 5 goals

Step 3: You now have two lists List A your top 5 items, and List B the 20 items you did not circle.

With these two lists are how you focus your week. The top five are your no matter what; these will be accomplished. The other 20 items are avoid-at-all-cost. This method is great because it forces those hard decisions and eliminating things that are not worthy of our valuable time commodity. It is all about finding a way to push you to narrow your focus and eliminate distractions.

So how do you push your attention span further to maintain focus? The biggest way high performers do this is by measuring their progress. It is easy to lose focus to face with there is a lack of feedback. Our brain has a natural craving to know about progression. High performers understand that it is impossible to know if they are progressing without feedback. This means they understand that there must be a way to measure results.

When we measure things, we maintain focus and concentration. As well when we measure things, those are the things that we see the greatest improvement on. High performers understand that with numbers and clear tracking that they have a greater understanding of if they are getting better or need improvement. Many standard performers fear to track performance because they are afraid of failing. The numbers tell the story, the trick that high performers understand is

Measurement about where you are, not who you are. High performers measure to understand, find out, and discover all kinds of things in their lives. The measure to see if they are spending time on a thing that provides value. With measuring, they find that they can focus on all the things that matter or provide value and ignore the things that do not.

High performers also understand that to access long-term focus, and they have to concentrate on the process, not the events. It is easy to have success at a single event and feel achievement and complete. People who want to be healthy see things as a means to an end. If I lose 20 pounds, then I will be fit. High performers see things differently; they understand that the process is more important than the event. In this example, the process is losing the weight the event is accomplishing, losing 20 pounds. It becomes a category of success in a single event. High performers take it to the next level by staying focused on the goals. The goal would be to stay fit, not just lose 20 pounds. They are committed to the process and practice daily, not just for a single event.

High performers know the process to stay focus on goals, and many use some tricks to improve their concentration. They begin by using anchor tasks. An anchor task is a single priority. This is the one non-negotiable thing that must be done each day. It is the priority. They use this anchor task because no matter the distraction that arises, they know that this will hold the rest of the day to the task. It forces them to focus the day around that task and be responsible for completion.

High performers are also experts at the management of their energy. They know that if a task requires the need for 100% attention, they schedule it at a time that they have full energy to focus. Many creative high performers use the morning as their time to focus because their energy is the highest in the morning. So they schedule their creativity task first thing in the morning. Allowing all other things to be taken care of in the afternoon. They understand that if you do not have the energy to put forth the effort, then all the time in the world is useless.

Focus is about removing distractions; high performers do not check their email first thing. Email can be the biggest distraction of all. When they push off checking email, they find that they can spend more time staying on the task rather than falling victim to someone else's agenda. This is a big win because they are not wasting energy digging through messages. As well they often stash their phone away. Leaving it in a different room or putting it in a draw on silent. It is much easier to focus on a task without the distractions of alerts, phone calls, or text messages interrupting your focus. While this may not be possible in all positions, try to find the time where you can carve out dedicated focus time.

Another tip high performer's use is to work in full-screen mode. When they work on their computer, they use full-screen mode. This allows them only to see the thing they are working on. There are no other distractions on their screen. They hide their menu bar and work fully on their projects. They have found that when you see the icon for different things, you are distracted and click on them. By working in a full-screen mode, they remove that distraction and are able to concentrate better.

High performers also focus on the most important thing first. This allows them to knock out the priority and frees them for any urgencies that may creep in later in the day. The biggest key is to reduce distractions to increase concentration and focus.

Habit 6 – Know Influence

High performers recognize that there are many different types of influence people can have. They use many different techniques to influence people to accomplish what they need from them. For a high performer, the concept of influence is a form of power that they possess. To better understand how they use power, it is important to understand the six different types of power. These powers are divided into categories of formal and informal power. Formal power includes coercive, reward, and positional power. The informal powers include expert, referent, and networking powers.

The first formal power is coercive power. This power is a focus of using one's ability to punish or take something away for failure to comply. People with this power often are those in control of firing employees. This is the least likely way that high performers act. People do not like coercive actions; thus, the reason there are very few successful dictators.

In contrast to coercive power is reward power. This power is the ability to reward a person. Anyone can actually use reward power. This is because reward power can come in many forms from bonuses, to public praise. The greatest success is found when the reward is scarce. Meaning it is hard to come by or achieve. People often are willing to do additional things in order to achieve scarce rewards. The third type of formal power is positional power. This is the power that one has simply from the position or title in an organization. It is quite similar to coercive power, those using this power do so simply because employees have respect for the position. It is simple people have more respect for the vice president of a company than they do the software engineering manager. Other examples would be a police officer; they have can arrest people, or a teacher assigns the grades for a class. These are all positions that can derive power from simply the role they hold.

The types of informal power differ and are expert referent and networking. Those who use expert power are skilled or knowledgeable in their field. They use their experiences, skills, or knowledge to make themselves the person to go to. These people do not necessarily have to hold any specific position in the company. Yet they can be quite influential in the success the company experiences. They often have the respect of their peers, simply based on their knowledge. The next type of power is referent; those with this power possess characteristics of a person that people respect, like, and even aspire to be like. Referent power can also be known as charisma. This is just the ability to gain the attention and admiration of others. These people do not earn power from the position; often, it is their uncanny ability to provide solutions and advice based on their likeability. The final power is networking; this is often the most underappreciated power. This power grows from investing in growing an extensive professional and personal network. These are the people who know exactly who to put others in touch with to get the solution to the problem. These people not only have all the right connections but often possess photographic memory capable of remembering each person's strengths and weaknesses of their networks. There is a great power that can be sourced from the ability to connect people.

It isn't what you have, or who you are, or where you are, or what you are doing that makes you happy. It what you think about it. –Dale Carnegie

---

So what is influence if not a form of power? Starting at infancy, we are working to influence others. To get the things we need or want. As we grow, these transition into goals, as crying and tantrums are looked down upon in the workplace. High performers understand that there are many techniques to use to achieve their goals. These techniques or tactics are distinguished as influence tactics. High performers also understand that there are different responses to attempts of influence. These responses are commitment, compliance, and resistance. The commitment response is when the influencer is able to get the target not simply to agree, but also actively provide support. This actually helps the performer get things done and keeps the vision alive. The compliance response is simply the influencer getting the person to agree not because they want to, but because they have to. Lastly, the resistance response happens with the influencers meet those that do not wish to comply. This resistance can be met as passive or actively rejecting the high performers attempt to influence. To meet each of these responses, high performers use tactics to influence outcomes. The more tactics a high performer has to gain influence, the greater the chances of overcoming the negative responses they may encounter.

The first tactic is rational persuasion, this tactic uses logical arguments, with facts, and data to convince others that your point of view is best. This is actually the most common tactic and widely used at all performance levels. The next tactic is inspirational appeals. This tactic taps into a person's beliefs, emotions, or values to gain support. A great example of this is how President John F. Kennedy said, "Ask not what your country can do for you; ask what you can do for your country." This iconic quote appealed to an entire nation of people's higher self-asking them to think bigger and outside of their own lives and for the nation. Those who are effective at this tactic are big-thinking, enthusiastic, personal, and, most importantly, authentic. Consultation is another tactic used. With this tactic, the influencer uses a democratic approach to decision making, allowing others to help or influence the group directly. The next tactic is ingratiation; this is simply making others feel good about themselves. Often influencers who use this tactic use a form of flattery. The goal is to establish themselves in good favor with the person they are trying to influence. Another tactic is personal appeal; this is a commonly used tactic. Personal appeal is influence gained because the person knows and likes you. Those that are influenced in this way have a specific level of comfort and familiarity. Exchange is also a tactic to influence people. Through the exchange, the influencer uses a give and take method. It is the most basic rule of reciprocation, which is repaid in kind what anyone has provided you. Often with this tactic, the influencer will give a small gift in the hope that the future will pay off. A study showed that a group of subjects were all given a Coke. Later the subjects were all asked to buy raffle tickets. Of those who received the drink, they bought twice as many raffle tickets than those who did not receive a drink. All of these are tactics to increase one's influence over a situation. The more tools the high performer possess, the greater the opportunity to influence the outcome they desire.

High performers also realize that they become like the top five people they spend the most time with. Research has shown that people start behaving like the, looking like them, and even making decisions based on what they believe and think. High performers recognize that they need people in their close circle that challenge them to be better. Some people think being the smartest person in the room is the best thing; however, it actually could be hurting you. High performers realize that they need to surround themselves with those who challenge them and are exceptional in many ways.

Take a moment and think about the five people you spend the most time with. Now assign each of the ma value from 1 to 10. Think about how each one affects your life. Do they elevate your thinking performance? High performers realize that those they are surrounded with a need to have a positive influence on their life. They should elevate thinking and push you to higher performance. Now, as you journey through life, it is understandable that your five can change or evolve. This is often because you are growing and changing. Quite honestly, the hardest part is critiquing the people you are around. This often can feel ruthless or judgmental. What separates high

Performers is they understand the influence on performance is critical to their success. They approach life that there is too much at stake to allow their five to hinder vision, energy, and ultimately their success.

Now, let me be clear; I am not saying throw all your people away and start over with new ones. You are not going to change your family, your church, and your parents. The people you spend time with often is somewhat flexible, and somewhat static. So changing who physically spend the most time with may not change easily. However, who you intellectually spend time with can. High performers identify who they can learn from, who they want to be like. They then focus on finding those people. This could be the top person in their field of work or industry.

Some high performers change their top five by who they listen to in podcasts. This allows them to be mentally with those top- level people that are driving success. Virtually becoming friends and getting to know about them. When high performers select their top five, they focus on four basic characteristics. First, they seek out people who are encouraging and positive. These people approach life with a positive outlook. Next, they look for those who encourage them to grow and think. High performers realize that there is not a neutral. You are either growing or reversing. Often these people are excellent conversationalists. The cause the people they are with to think about things in a way that stretches and refines personal views. This helps the performer with their problems solving skills. High performers also look for those interested in helping them to achieve their goals. If someone in your five is a hindrance to your goals, it is time to have a hard conversation with yourself. You need people around you that want you to succeed. Finally, your five should include people who encourage, inspire, and motivate you to be more. If people in your circle want to see you level up, you begin to feel a sense of pride. You level up not just intellectually, but physically, emotionally, and spiritually. High performers understand that those they are with are the greatest influence on their success. So be with great people and level up your game!

Habit 7 – Push Beyond Comfort

High performers understand the meaning behind all those inspirational messages telling them to push the limits. To get out of their comfort zones. They see the potential of something new that helps prevent them from experiencing burn out and that it can be good for their brain. Yet when just starting, it can be hard to change take that leap. This is because the comfort zone is a behavioral space, a safe place where your activities and behaviors fit into a pattern to minimize risk and stress. It provides a type of mental security blanket. Within this zone, you feel low anxiety, less stress, and happiness. The concept of the comfort zone dates back to an experiment conducted in 1908. Where subjects were found to have a steady

Level of performance when they were relatively comfortable. However, high performers understand that there is an optimal level of anxiety needed to get out of the comfort zone and into maximum performance. They also understand that too much anxiety causes excess stress to be produce, and performance drops off sharply. This is why high performers try to stay in balance, in the sweet spot if you will.

For many, they are not pushing themselves as much as they could. Even when they have to reach the goal. They typically are setting goals that they know they can reach while staying in their comfort zones. This inhibits their growth. High performers understand that there is a necessity to push beyond these areas to reach full potential. Here are some attributes that they get by stepping out of their comfort zone and reach their optimal anxiety zone where experiences peak performance and mental productivity.

Confidence is a necessary attribute of a high performer. As they reach optimal anxiety, they become more confident. Many spend their life wishing they could be someone else, wishing they could do more, or believe in their abilities more. What separates the high performers is that they have come to the realization that they can be the person they aspire to be. They understand that their goals are safe and that they require work, but they also get that there is a risk to attain these goals. They have found that the more they push themselves, the more they realize just how capable they are of the impossible. They find that situations they would have previously had anxiety in they now are comfortable, and feel more self-assured.

Creditability is another thing that high performers gain by stepping out of their comfort zones. Regardless of how uncomfortable a high performer is, they understand that they cannot allow apprehension or hesitation with others. They understand that when you do, you stifle your potential. A great example of this is doing something for the first time. Maybe it is public speaking. The high performer taps back into their belief. That they must believe in themselves. While the first experience may be slightly awkward, they understand that there are people who want the information. So they must reach out with creditability and share it.

High performers say yes to opportunities, regardless of any intimidation factors. They understand that an opportunity to grow lies within each experience. There are values in learning through experience that cannot be taught in a book or classroom. High performers understand that dealing with change is necessary. That through unexpected change, great growth can occur. They also understand that pretending uncertainty and fear do not exist the worst thing someone can do. This is why they use controlled risks and challenges to gain experience. Learning to live in their optimal anxiety zone can be life-changing.

The world of technology has created a largely introverted society. People love being alone and struggle with making new connections. They love the idea of connecting with people, but actually making it happen is hard. However, it is pushing out of our phones and into real relationships with people that we can find greater strength. These connections are the ones that will help to grow your vision, the network that will provide support. High performers understand that making new contacts, learning new skills, and interests help you become a versed person. The force themselves to get out of their comfort zones and aspire for more than Netflix. At the end of the day, they understand that they are the only person who truly can hold back their success.

High performers understand that when you work within your comfort area, you are killing productivity. Those who procrastinate and wait until the deadline to finish something enhance their productivity by 50%. Now I am not saying to procrastinate. I am saying set deadlines and expectations. When you drive yourself to achieve the day's goals, you can hone in on those goals and increase productivity. It also prevents you from falling into the mentality of being busy. Busy will not always be equally productive and can also force you to avoid trying new things. Pushing boundaries helps you grow and get more done. For high performers, the beginning is difficult, but like anything else, it becomes easier over time. Living in your optimal anxiety will become a place where you feel normal, and pushing farther in your performance feels like success.

A soft benefit that high performers receive from getting out of their zone is it is easier to brainstorm and be creative. Seeking experiences opens the door to educate you in ways that little else can. Through trying new things, you are able to evaluate old ideas and asses where new knowledge can inspire greater success. Through seeing old problems in a new light, you are able to tackle the same challenge differently with renewed energy.

> Sever the ties to your comfort zone. Stretch yourself to see the wonders for you beyond the horizons. Get up on your tiptoes…great things await only those who see and believe. It's only them that can receive. – Manuela George-Izunwa

So how do you push beyond? First, you must remember that you only want to tip the scale slightly. We are talking about pushing out to controlled anxiety. Each person's comfort zone is different, and what may be optimal for one person can prove to be overboard for another. So let's look at a few ways to expand your comfort zone without going too far. Start by doing something different every day. This could be a small or large change. Just make a change in the way you do things day-to- day. Evaluate if the perspective of the event changed. If the perspective is negative, do not be put off, everything will not work out. When I talk of these simple day-to-day changes, they can be as small as trying a new restaurant or going vegetation for a week. The goal here is to recalibrate your reality.

Another way is to take time with your decision making. Slowing down the process can often be a huge hurdle. In society, we are honed to quick thinking and prize that is not just our work but also our personal lives. When you slow things down and take time to interpret and observe, you give yourself time to be educated about the situation. Things become more about thinking and less about reacting. Now, if you are a person that already is the type that weighs in on things before deciding, you may find that sometimes making a snap decision pushes you to optimal anxiety. These decisions can help you get moving; they are a sort of kick start for projects and teach you that you can trust your judgment.

Finally, stepping out of your zone takes courage, and you should not just go all out. Begin by stepping out in small steps. You will get the same benefit going small as you do jumping in. The big thing is not to be afraid to start. Start small and continue to challenge yourself.

High performers know that there are many ways they can stretch their personal boundaries. They connect with people they are inspired by, they volunteer for organizations they are passionate about. They travel, ultimately they work to broaden their perspectives in every way that they can. This does not mean to book that flight to Italy and buy leather shoes. No, it means to get out of your front door and experience things. The big picture is they are doing things. They are pushing themselves to get past their mental blocks and achieve things.

Chapter 4: Blueprint of Personal Change

One thing is certain and that we are currently living in an era of accelerating change. This can be seen in many aspects of relationships, business, life, and even politics. There are very few things that are constant and solid. It as if nearly every process is in a state of change, and you have to be prepared to move forward to thrive. Many people thrive in change, knowing how to adapt and cope in environments of change.

Personal change beings with the understanding that our references come from the collective memories of our life. Therefore, every act is based on our experiences. The goal of personal change is to develop our potential. It is the ultimate enhancer for a person's life. As we improve the experiences of our life, we also improve our lives. It is essential to understand then that improvement requires work, and work requires change.

When beginning personal change, it is important to understand that change is not easy. In fact, many efforts to change actually fail. One example of this is the fitness industry sees a huge influx of new memberships at the beginning of the year. Yet nearly 80% of those members drop off within 60 days. While our blueprint is no magic bullet, we have found those who use these processes see great results.

Vision without action is a dream. Action without vision is simply passing the time. Action with vision is making a positive difference. – Joel Barker

Define Change

To begin with, it is important to have a clear understanding of change. The first step is all about defining the change you would like to make. What is the purpose? Why is it important? The greater the power the change has in your life, the more likely you are to accomplish it successfully. It is important to be specific with these changes.

Plan

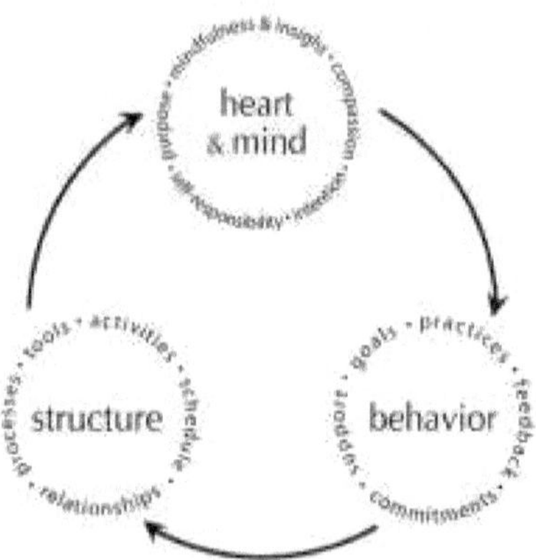

The approach for the plan is a system with a focus on a wheel of change. Changing the complex system of your life has a huge impact on you. This is because change requires us to realize all

of these things affect our thoughts, feelings, behavior, and environment. Using the wheel of change as a guide, you can integrate change in each of the three domains: heart-mind, behavior, and structural.

Let's first look at heart and mind. When beginning to change, we start with getting clear about our desire, concerns, and motivation. If we are clear on these, we are more likely to engage with changing the other parts of the circle. This is one of the biggest reasons we are not proponents of New Year's resolutions. The change should be deliberate and structured; this is the only way to stick with it long term. When you begin looking inside, it is important to understand that you are on a journey, not just heading towards a destination. Changing your programming is about also attending to your heart and mind.

So how do you begin to meet the needs of changing your heart and mind to promote personal change? Think of these things like a list of to-do. As well, understand that not all of these require being addressed with ever-changing, but they are tools for evaluating and promoting the changes you seek.

Purpose is the first concept. It is essential to connect with your purpose. This is the experience that gives you meaning to your life. Your purpose should be the one thing that guides you, as well as a great source of will power and wisdom. The stronger the WHY, the greater your motivation. The next is the intention. Why exactly do you want to align or create this change? You need to be able to deal with any uncertainty that seeks in your mind proactively. This will allow your heart-mind to gain power through the change. Which feeds into mindfulness. The change will most often require you to shift your mindset, to allow your heart to open to possibilities that you had not considered. It is with mindfulness that you can stay self-reflective regardless of what challenges are trying to derail your change. Self-compassion is the next concept. It is very easy to allow yourself to be driven by your inner critic. That voice inside your head that is chronically telling us what we should do or what we should not do. This voice can be harsh and actually encourage failure. If you miss a day, do not allow that inner voice to tell you that you have failed. Rather allow yourself to have compassion and understand that the process of change is a journey. Finally, self-responsibility is the last in our heart-mind model. It is easy to fall victim to the things that we feel. However, if you want to see a personal change, you have to take responsibility for the excuses you make. There may be obstacles you face, but you have to be prepared to meet them and overcome them. This begins by taking responsibility for the choices and mobilizing yourself to accomplish your goals.

The next area is behavior change; these changes are the foundation for growth. They also require shifts in habits and behavior, to change what we do not do and what we do accomplish. This begins with setting goals. We understand that our intentions are translated into outcomes and goals. This is the way that we realize the behaviors that need to change to achieve the goals. In setting milestones along the way to larger goals, we are able to track and stay motivated. Commitment plays an important role, as well. To succeed, we have to be specific, clear, and have do-able commitments. However, it is important only to make commitments that you are certain you will keep. This is a more skillful approach as it requires smaller and manageable commits to achieve change. Through sticking with the commitments, you build confidence and sustain motivation throughout the process. Practice is the next step; whether you realize it or not, you have been unconsciously practicing your entire life. These repetitions build strong Nero pathways and create habits. It is with practice that you can begin to change behavior. Practice should be deliberate and consciously done until the new change becomes a habit. Recognizing change also requires feedback. Feedback is needed regularly to help continue to move towards the goal. Personal change is harder for us to get feedback, but there are many creative ways you can track your progress. From using journaling to working with an accountability partner to hiring a coach. Which feeds into the last part of this section support. It is important to understand that you do not have to go through personal change alone. Creating new habits needs encouragement and support. Those most successful with achieving great personal change have a strong support system. This could be anything from their support network to their coat, to colleagues, or even workshops.

The final area of our circle is structure. This is the area that the environment impacts us. This is where we make the external changes to our life to sustained change. It is with a structural change that we support our new behaviors and feed our hearts and mind. The first part of this section is we evaluate the activities that either inhibit or support the change we want to make. We then look at what can empower the change process. The next section we look at is our schedule. Many feel that personally, they are a slave to their self. That their calendar is what controls their day, forgetting that they are the ones who decide what is on the calendar, not vice versa. If you want to change, we have to take the time and pace our life to make it happen. As well the people you are influenced by play a huge role in your ability to achieve personal change. It is essential to be conscious of this and create plans for change. This may include determining that certain relationships are inhibiting your ability to change. It is important to evaluate relationships and invest more time in those that support your change. Another aspect is your personal processes. What your routine looks like, how do you do your planning, what is your workflow like? How do you delegate? Taking a step back to examine the relevant processes can provide you with insight into how they are either supporting the change you desire or inhibiting it.

Here is an example of what the process is like in action:

Challenge – I need to increase my fitness level.

The plan:

Heart-Mind

- Self-reflection on why I have not been consistent with fitness.
- Reflect on what I can change this time
- Connect with the desire to exercise more than the feeling that I should do more.

Behavior

- Commit to a fitness class once a week
- Commit to a specific at home work out twice a week
- Engage a friend or partner to support these choices.

Heart-Mind

- Join a fitness center closer to home

- Download a workout plan for practice at home.

- Find a friend who will commit to working out with you, acknowledging that you do better with the company.

- Restructure your evening schedule to allow time for working out.

- Create a tracking chart to measure progress and track exercise commitments.

By using systematic approaches to change, you can create your very one virtue cycle. With each cog of the wheel provoking and reinforcing the others.

Develop Way to Tracking Progress

When deciding on your goal, it is essential also to consider how you will track that goal. How you can measure the progress, you make towards achieving it. These are just a few ways that you can make tracking your goal more tangible and feel a greater amount of success.

Using facts, the method of quantitative measurement is probably the most common practice. As you set your goals that alight with facts and figures. For many goals, he will be a process of signing a numeric value to the goal. There are many quantitative ways to measure success, and this is one of the quickest ways you can see a progression. The next way is to stay on plan. Within your plan, you may have challenges that you were able to overcome relatively quickly. While your main goal still requires work. Staying on the plan allows you to break each part of the goal down and set mini-goals or milestones for success. As well it forces you to adhere to a timeframe and track your progress alongside that timeframe. Sticking to the time frame is important, but do not forget to forgive yourself by allowing flexibility in your plan. This also means understanding that the plan may need to change as you progress. Record keeping is also a great way to track your progress; this is not simply quantitative data but personal notes as well. This will give you something to refer back to should you fail to meet your target. As well, when you exceed a goal, it will provide you a road map to follow for potential future success. Another option is creating checklists. This is a great way to track the achievement of your goals. As tasks are completed, simply checking them off creates a feeling of confidence and success. Through using these checklists, you can quickly review how successful you were at following the plan and be able to recognize patterns of where you may be struggling to adhere. Finally, always rate your progress. This is the best way to track goals that are otherwise not quantitative in the capture, like increasing your confidence. Measuring these goals is as simple as deciding a system, a numeric system of 1-5 is an effective approach. With this approach, you would honestly rate your confidence rate on the scale. Then you can plot your scores to provide yourself a graphical visualization of the progress. Regardless of the method, you use the key to this step is finding a system that will work best for you. Then committing to stick with the system.

Trak and Adjust

The last thing that you do is implementation, tracking, and adjusting. The most important thing to remember is the vision or goal that you want the personal change for. Allowing that to be the guiding light as you journey through your personal change.

Using a weekly process for assessing your progress is a great way to provide yourself feedback on the success you are making. While you are working daily to track the progress, you are making towards your goal. The idea is that you are honest with yourself and the reference point of which your goal is currently at. This provides you with vital information to see how you are able to progress forward and also if you need to adjust the plan.

Another method is setting up a monthly personal review. The idea is to review your goal monthly and see the progress you have made towards change. This could be a scheduled meeting where you take time to evaluate and negotiate what you need to enhance or adjust your change. The great thing about this is the review of change is often personal and requires time to see the traction. Allowing yourself the time to evaluate is essential in long term growth and personal change.

The following is a blueprint example that will help you work through your own ideas of personal change. By using this blueprint, you can begin to translate your desire into an actionable real plan; you can increase the likelihood of success, gain confidence, and feel a personal change.

Step 1 – Define what the change is

- Why is this change important to you?
- What is the purpose of the change?
- What do you desire to be different?
- What outcomes are you expecting?

Step 2 – Plan using the wheel of the change process

- Heart-Mind
- Behavior
- Structure

Step 3 – Develop ways to track your progress

Step 4 – Track your progress and evaluate the needs for change.

Desired Change	
P: The Purpose This is why this goal is important to you.	
O: The Outcome What is the outcome you desire? What is it that you desire to be different?	

P: The Process - How you will implement change.	
Heart-Mind: • What is required to shift the way I feel and think?	
Behavior: • What needs to change about the ways I act?	
Structure: • What external changes must I make to my environment?	
I will track my progress by:	

Example: Becoming more fit.

Desired Change	Increasing my fitness level
P: The Purpose This is why this goal is important to you.	I want to have more energy and better health.
O: The Outcome What is the outcome you desire? What is it that you desire to be different?	• Regular exercise plus lower body mass index. • Have more energy, and be proud of my body.
P: The Process - How you will implement change.	
Heart-Mind: What is required to shift the way I feel and think?	• Self-reflection on why I have not been consistent with fitness.

	• Reflect on what I can change this time
	• Connect with the desire to exercise more than the feeling that I should do more.
Behavior: What needs to change about the ways I act?	• Commit to a fitness class once a week • Commit to a specific at home work out twice a week • Engage a friend or partner to support these choices.
Structure: What external changes must I make to my environment?	• Join a fitness center closer to home • Download a workout plan for practice at home. • Find a friend who will commit to working out with you, acknowledging that you do better with the company. • Restructure your evening schedule to allow time for

	working out. • Create a tracking chart to measure progress and track exercise commitments.
I will track my progress by:	• Minimum workouts of 3 each week • Start with one fitness class at gym week 2, then move to multiple classes by week 4 • Track workouts on my calendar • Review and progress monthly with BMI measurement and energy rating of 1 - 5

Chapter 5: Reaching Success in Life Under All Aspects

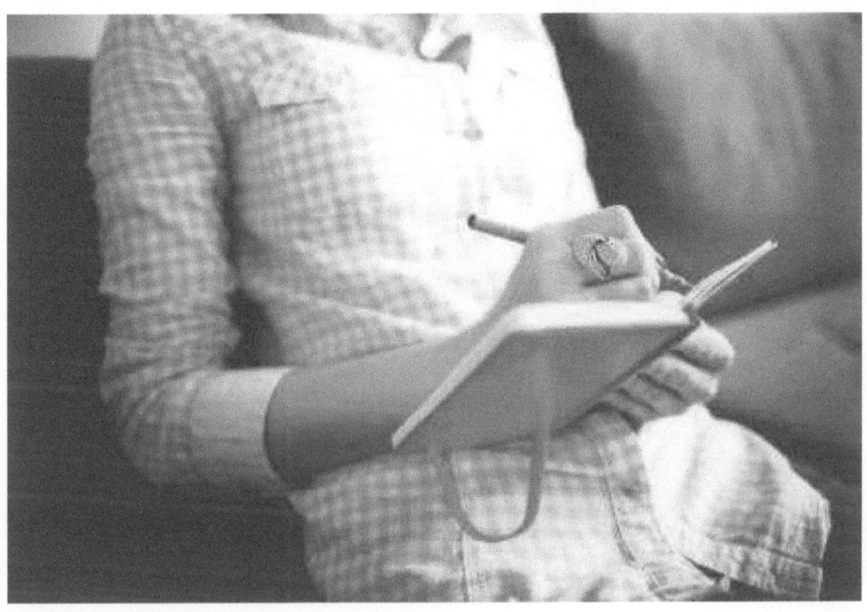

Many people spend their entire life trying to figure out the mystery of success and honestly never figure it out. Those who want success learn that there are keys to find it, those that do not live a life often with a victim mentality. The truth is you have to have the desire to succeed; you cannot think that success will simply fall into your lap. Those who desire success want to be happy; they want to have a career they enjoy; they want to achieve financial independence. They want to be significant in some way on those around them and the world.

One important thing to understand is that you do not have to figure it all out. Honestly, trying to solve all the mysteries alone of success would be a waste of your time. Many had come before you and laid the groundwork so that you can follow the paths they have and learn from their mistakes.

So quite often the least path of resistance to success is finding out what others have done and following their processes. Learning from their systems and mistakes saves you time.

Success is a wonderful thing; it tends to have a snowball effect. That is achieving one goal, then rolls into another and another, and before you know it, you have developed yourself a program for success. The more one achieves, the more you grow, and so do your achievements. With each success, you build confidence and believe in yourself that the next time a challenge arises, you can succeed. This allows you to leverage your achievement for momentum to personal success and reach those ultimate visions. Those truly vested in success are able to create a synergistic effect and unleash their ultimate potential.

Unleashing potential is possible for anyone; the only limit is what you can do. What you are selfoimposed to do or believe you can do. You have to make the decision to release yourself from your mental limitations and put yourself 100% into accomplishing your greatest goals.

Time-Limited Goals

We already understand that to achieve the goals. You have to write them down and create a plan. But it is also necessary to set a deadline to meet them. The reason deadlines have a great effect is because they create a sense of urgency. They help you to finish the project or reach a goal. They also help to break up the goal into a series of tasks allowing the ultimate goal to be more achievable. As well when you break the goals up, you prevent yourself form waiting until the last minute to finish all the work. Which, for some goals, is impossible, you cannot wait to lose 10 pounds the day before your big meeting.

Once you have those tasks figured out, then you need to come up with an organized deadline for each goal. These I like to call mini-goals; they all lead you to achieve your ultimate goal. Think of it like this, you cannot have a war without battles, and you cannot win the war without winning any battles.

Here are some tips for using deadlines to achieve your goals.

1. To prevent procrastination, set up each step on your calendar, and assign a notification to ensure you do not miss deadlines.
2. Writing down your goals is a proven method of achieving them as well; assigning a deadline in writing also subconsciously makes that deadline more concrete, and thus you more committed.
3. Set time limits for your tasks; if you know that you can do something in 30 minutes, don't set an hour for the task. The objective is to work as efficiently as possible.
4. A timer can be useful to help you keep track of tasks you are working on and prevent you from working to slowly. It also lets you know when it is time to change tasks.
5. Always pick the hardest thing to do first. This way, you exert the most energy on difficult things. It also allows you to wrap up the easy things, in the end, making the project go more quickly.
6. Have a contingency plan for if you miss a deadline. This plan should include how you are going to deal with the inevitable curveball that gets thrown your way.
7. Support, support, support. Sharing your deadlines with people helps to hold you accountable. This is where your coach, accountability partner, or spouse can help keep you honest with your deadlines.

Plan Short Term Easy Victories

With the knowledge that significantly many efforts to change fail, it is important to implement a successful system. This is a new type of quality control to compensate you with quick wins to keep you focused on the long term goal. AS you are journeying through change, remember that there is resistance. Yet, nothing shifts momentum like a victory. With planning short term targets that are easy to hit along your journey, you will build success. The key to change is being able to set sail in that direction, even when the wind is blowing hard.

Start by going all out to share the small wins, do not be tempted to overlook the first objective of your goal being accomplished. Take time and be grateful that you made it past that first challenge and share that with your support system. When it comes to victories, it is not the time to be modest. It is time to remind yourself of what it took to get to that point. This builds your confidence and ability to impact change. This also builds the charge to achieve your next challenge and propels you forward to feel the same level of success again. It is also important to note the hardships you had to overcome to access the change. Change is not easy, so acknowledgment of the pains it took to get to the next level can have a major impact on your moral. As you achieve victory, it is also important to then go back and analyze the shits. What happened during this change? What made it successful? What made it more challenging?

Then learning from these analyzations will help you be better prepared as you go into the next challenge. Use your wins to remove those who do not support your success. The resisters to success will become obvious as you grow. Weeding these people out of your inner circle allows you to continue to foster change and grow. And finally, shift your thinking from neutral to vested. As you are more and more vested in the changes and achieving small victories, you will continue to grow in success.

A final victory is an accumulation of many short-term encounters. To lightly dismiss a success because it does not usher in a complete order of justice is to fail to comprehend the process of achieving full victory. – Martin Luther King, Jr.

Celebrate

There is a small community in Canada that takes a very different approach with its police department. They have an initiative that is handing out positive tickets to young people. If they see someone crossing the street correctly or cleaning up litter, they "ticket" the person with a positive ticket. The tickets include free food, movie tickets, and sometimes hockey game seats. This is a very innovative way to approach dealing with crime. Rather than passing harsher laws, they found a way to encourage better behaviors. As a result, crime in youths has reduced by an astonishing 65%.

It is quite easy to push ourselves to continue bad behaviors. It really comes naturally, and often, we don't feel guilty right away that it might lead to poor performance. Like staying up to late and not allowing your body to rest before work the next day. However, for some reason, we are not typically equipped to bring out the incentives. It is common for when we make a small mistake to feel poorly about it. Yet, when we accomplish a small goal, we nearly never feel great about the accomplishment. This is a big problem as there is not a balance between negative and positive feelings.

This is why small wins are so very important to our success. Through tracing our successes, we boost our sense of confidence. When you unlock the ability to leverage that confidence, you can push yourself to have greater success. This actually comes down to a very biological response. The neurotransmitter dopamine is released when we feel good. This is the chemical that enables us to feel the sweet reward of success and trigger happiness.

However, many feel silly about celebrating small wins. That these victories are not substantial enough to note achievement. They often do not see the bigger picture of celebrating the fact that they made it to the gym. The thing is they are not celebrating the achievement, but you are celebrating that you are changing your habits. You are pushing yourself to different behaviors and becoming the change that you want to see. It is through reinforcing good behavior that we develop an addiction to the process and can reach even higher goals. Ultimately you are creating a habit of success. Habits can be hard to adapt, and therefore when you celebrate their success, you increase your motivation. You become appreciative of the small things. Appreciating these little wins can make the greatest difference between success and failure. The lack of gratefulness can lead you down a path that is hard to come back from. However, celebrating those small successes allows you to acknowledge that you are on the right path that you can, in fact, achieve the goals and dreams you have laid out for yourself.

Fail With Forgiveness

Very few people can look back at their life and see nothing but perfect choices and decisions. Many will see things from small failures to colossal mistakes. Failure can be painful, earth-shattering, and monumental. Through these experiences, it is easy to question how you could forgive yourself. To begin to question your very existence.

The truth of the matter is that failure is part of life and necessary. Failure teaches more lessons than you may realize. Failure is the natural way of helping us move to different levels and learn from experiences. While failure provides a great service to us in the long term. At the moment, it can be hard to see past it. It can drain our enthusiasm, energy, and drive us to give up on our goals. When you allow failure to become attached to your emotions, it has the potential to ruin you completely.

Failing with forgiveness is a shift in your perspective. This allows you to shift the source of the failure form a negative emotion to a positive learning experience. The first thing you have to realize is it is okay to fail. It is not okay to give up on yourself. With failure, you must forgive yourself no matter what. You must understand that you can move forward from here and define the experience. The greater the failure, the more you have to learn. With failure, we are forced to look inward and seek a deeper meaning. You must realize that many of the most famous people have failed. The thing that separates them is they get back up and try again, and again.

One thing to remember is that you are deserving of forgiveness. If your closest friend came to you with a story of how they failed. You most often would offer advice and comfort to them. Chances are you would encourage them to not be so hard on yourself. So if we are willing to do that for others, why are we not willing to provide ourselves with the same forgiveness? This is because deep down, our inner self needs to be treated like our friend. You need to understand that your inner self is fragile and that your ego can suffer when you fail. Often this requires you to make it clear to yourself that you are forgiven in order to move past the failure.

One of the greatest challenges we have is we set our self-up for our own demise. We think that success is easy to come by. We seek instant gratification as a result of our on-demand society. Where everything we want is simply right at our fingertips. This makes it hard for us to understand the challenges that success cannot happen on-demand. In truth, we have to be willing to put in the work to achieve our goals. We have to accept the failures and learn to grow. One lesion is it becomes easy to realize that if you truly want something, you can forgive yourself for any failure. Thomas Edison is a great example; it took him over 10,000 times to create the lightbulb. If he had given up because of his failure, where would we be?

> I didn't fail – I just learned 9,000 ways not to make a light bulb. – Thomas Edison

Failures can help to redefine our perspectives and provide clarity and understanding about the changes needing to happen in our life. As you learn to forgive yourself for failure, you will unleash yourself to greater success.

Use Metrics to Recognize Success

One of the greatest mistakes people use is the wrong metrics for misusing their success. They look to measure the wrong things, not they may specifically rely on quantitative data and not take into account the qualitative data. Keeping metrics simple is a way to keep them on track. One key factor is to ensure you do not overwhelm yourself with data, nor do you provide yourself with information that provides overconfidence. While yes, you need to have the confidence to be successful, there is danger in overconfidence. When you are overconfident, you push yourself to continue to drive performance in one direction with our care for the results of success. This is why you have to use metrics to drive your success. All the confidence in the world will help if you are are not putting your efforts in the right place.

As you journey on your path to your goals, it is important to realize that you must revisit your metrics regularly. Successful people understand that priorities can change as you progress towards your goal. They see the power invalidating the ways they measure their success. This also means that they must be able to shift their strategy. Yet, they must remember that any shifts in strategy require changes to the metrics in which they are measured. Ultimately ensuring that the outcomes and behaviors align with the changes to the plan. As well using success metrics are the best way to view improvement. This is because you can see the needle moving.

Measuring how you feel about your goal is part of measuring your success. Are you lifting up to your goals? Is your personal change happening the way you expected? What are your behaviors telling you about the change? The bottom line is you have to know where you are going and measure your growth to get there. As well, you have to understand that the achievement of your success takes time, and you can get there if you continue to grow, re-evaluate, and perform.

Not everything that counts can be counted, and not everything that can be counted, counts. – Albert Einstein

Conclusion

Congratulations, you made it to the end of The 5 Habits of High-Performance People. You are now equipped with an arsenal of knowledge on how to level up your life. I hope it was informative and able to provide you with great new tools you need to achieve your goals, whatever they are. As you dive into accessing all the concepts in this book, you will unlock new performance levels. It is with the understanding of how high performers acquire success; you can begin to open your mind to any possibility.

The next step on your journey to a greater understanding begins with looking inside yourself. What is your vision? What do you wish to improve in the world? How can you change your attitude in everyday life? It is okay to be unable to answer these questions as you are just beginning your journey to the next level. Or you simply are wanting to learn more about ways to level up your game. Even if you decide that the path of the high performer is not the one you for you at this moment. Understand that using some of the simple practices in this book within your everyday life can help to improve yourself. Allow yourself to act in kindness through your everyday activities. Taking time to go into your days with greater care. To prepare yourself for challenges you might face, and rather than being reactive, be proactive. Give yourself the gift of permission, to fail forward and empower those who you work with. Freeing yourself of negativity and unleash your possibilities.

Finally, if you found this book useful in any way, a review on Amazon is always appreciated!

Printed by Libri Plureos GmbH in Hamburg,
Germany